YOU HAVE WHAT IT TAKES

What Every Father Needs to Know

JOHN ELDREDGE

NELSON BOOKS
A Division of Thomas Nelson Publishers
Since 1798

Published in Nashville, Tennessee, by Thomas Nelson, Inc.

Published in association with Yates & Yates, LLP, Attorneys
and Counselors, Orange, California.

ISBN 0-7394-4323-2

Printed in the United States of America

To my father

CONTENTS

THE SECRET TO BOYS

Every little boy is asking one basic question.

You notice it in nearly everything he does.

Little boys love *adventure*. Just the other day my wife was having a cup of coffee in the kitchen when she saw—out of the corner of her eye—something fly out the second-story window. She investigated and found a rope, made of bedsheets, hanging from the boys' bedroom window. They had stripped their beds, knotted the sheets together, anchored the "rope" to their bunk beds, and were rappelling down the side of the house, Batman style. Just a typical Saturday morning in a house of boys.

Give a little guy a bicycle. Is it enough that he learns to ride it? Of course not. As soon as those training wheels are off (no, sooner), he's seeing how *fast* it can go, riding with no hands, jumping it off the curb, making skid marks on the sidewalk, racing against all comers. Noises go with it, too, noises that no one needs to teach a boy—he just knows how to make them. Loud engine noises and speedy, whooshing noises and screeching, crashing noises and a soundtrack to go with it all. That is no mere bike he's riding, and he is no mere boy. He's a motorcycle racer, a fighter pilot, a starship captain.

Look at the stories boys love, the games they play. They are full of battle and adventure and danger. They love to build things . . . and then blow 'em up. They love to jump off stuff. What does a boy wear if you let him wear what he *wants* to wear? Let him out of his school clothes and his Sunday school togs, and in a moment he'll be decked out in camouflage, army style, or dressed up as a cowboy, a fireman, a superhero, a Jedi knight with a bath towel wrapped around him and a stern look in his eye. Every boy wants to be a hero. Every boy wants to be powerful, he wants to be dangerous, and he wants to know: *Do I have what it takes?*

That's the question every boy is asking: "Do I have what it takes?"

And when he grows a bit older, it turns to fast cars (the louder, the better), computer games of battle and adventure, and making the sports team. He wants to hit the home run in the bottom of the ninth. He wants to make a slam dunk just before the buzzer sounds. If he's more academically inclined, well, then, he wants to win at chess; he wants to ace the test; he wants to come out on top.

He wants to prove himself. And all through those years, when he's riding his bike with no hands or trying to look cool and doing all those other things that boys do, *he is looking to impress you.*

Because every boy shares the same basic question: "Do I have what it takes?"

And every boy looks to his dad to answer it.

THE SECRET TO GIRLS

Every little girl is asking one basic question too. But it's a very different question.

You can observe it there in nearly everything *she* does. Little girls typically don't invent games where bloodshed is a prerequisite for having fun, where large numbers of people "die" as a regular part of the routine. On the other hand, boys don't love to brush each other's hair. They don't go to tea parties (unless they are dragged into them by their sisters). Sitting down over make-believe china, being very polite, and having "grown-up" conversations make the party an entirely feminine affair. It's all part of those relational games that girls create. Boys may have invented hockey, but little girls invented games like "wedding day" and "mommies and daddies" and "rescue the princess." You don't have to teach them to do it—it comes naturally. It's part of their design.

This is *not* to say that girls dislike adventure. They love to climb trees and make mud pies and all that. Many girls love to play sports. But there is something profoundly different between little boys and little girls. Watch them on a rainy day. Trapped inside the house, boys make up games like "terrorize the cat" and "urban commando." Girls cuddle and care for a favorite doll or stuffed animal, or they dress up the family puppy. Speaking of "dress up," that was a feminine creation as well. Give a group of girls a chest of gowns and shoes and Mom's costume jewelry, and they are captured for hours playing "princess" and "movie star" and generally being beautiful.

For her question is very different from that of her brothers. Every little girl wants to know: *Am I lovely?*

And when she grows a bit older, she talks on the phone for hours and wants to know who is dating whom. While the guy is clueless about what to wear to the prom, it is a *very* big deal for a young woman. She watches shows about relationships, pores over fashion magazines and bridal magazines, and loves to get cards and flowers from a secret admirer. Why are flowers such a big deal for women? I have been sent flowers once in my life, and I thought it was weird. But my wife loves to get flowers. Have you ever wondered why? Because of what it says. *I'm thinking of you . . . I delight in you.* All through those years, when she's dressing up and doing shows for you and playing princess and trying to look beautiful and shedding tears over the fact that she might not be, *she is trying to capture your attention.*

She wants to know: *Am I lovely?* That's the question every little girl is asking. And she looks to her dad to answer it.

WHAT A FATHER
NEEDS TO DO

I'm going to make fathering very simple: answer your child's question.

Answer, "Yes, you have what it takes," or "Yes, you are lovely."

Answer it a thousand times in a thousand ways over the course of your son's or daughter's life, and you will have done your job. You will have hit a home run. You don't need a Ph.D. in child psychology to be a dad. It isn't rocket science. Understand what a little boy and a little girl need to hear from their dad; understand each one's question. Then answer it intentionally, answer it with love, and you will have offered the best a father can give.

Oh, and it's not just little boys and girls, either. Your son or daughter, no matter how old, will always want and need to hear those words from you. To a son: "You have what it takes. You are a man." To a daughter: "You are lovely. You are worth fighting for." This will remain true for the rest of each one's life.

THE MOST POWERFUL
MAN IN THE WORLD

Just the other day my ten-year-old son, Luke, snuggled up to me after dinner as I was reading in my chair, and he said, with big eyes and a sweet face, "Dad . . . can I ask you a question?"

I knew he was after something. Cookies maybe. Or permission to run down to a friend's house. "Sure," I said. "What's up?"

"Dad . . . can I have a chain saw?"

The things these boys come up with. It cracks me up. He was dead serious, by the way.

You understand. We all—as men—pretty much want the same thing. We want power. We want to have an impact. We want to leave our mark on the world. A boy with a chain saw is a powerful thing. Just imagine all he could do. In a short time there wouldn't be a tree left standing in the entire neighborhood. Which, of course, is why I did not give him one. A ten-year-old with a chain saw is more powerful than he ought to be. But I understand the desire. It's essential to the masculine nature.

Boys who play baseball don't want to strike out. They want to hit that ball hard. They want to knock it over the fence. My boys love to wrestle with me, but they don't simply want to wrestle—they want to pin me. They want to be on top. This is true of every man. This is what's behind men and their fascination with fast cars, or power tools, or politics. It's about *power*. When they grow up, they wear power ties and have power lunches. A man may take it in the wrong direction sometimes, but the bottom line is, a man needs to know he's having an impact.

Or think of it this way: What's your worst fear as a man? Isn't it some version of *failure*? To royally blow it? To really screw things up? Lose your job. Drive your company into bankruptcy. Wind up pushing a shopping cart down the street. If you're a doctor, you fear misdiagnosing a patient's fatal disease. If you're an attorney, you fear losing the big case. Because all those things in some way prove that you *don't* have what it takes.

Not so for a woman. A woman's worst fear is *abandonment*. Most women survive a career setback that would send men into a tailspin. Failure doesn't seem to matter as much because a woman fears that she won't be *loved*. It shouts to the world, "She wasn't worth pursing; she wasn't worth fighting for." But for men, the dog at our heels is failure.

We need to know that our lives mattered. That when the time came, we had what was needed. We came through. There was something powerful about our lives.

So let me say this as clearly as I can: You, Dad, are the most powerful man in the world . . . at least in their world. Your children are looking to you to answer the deepest question of their lives. How you handle their hearts will shape them for the rest of their lives. Never forget that no one is as powerful as you are in the lives of your sons and daughters.

Please note that I am not saying Mom is unimportant. Not at all. Mother teaches us unconditional love, and she teaches us about mercy. She is a comforter. When boys or girls want to do something adventurous, they don't ask Mom; they ask Dad. But when they skin their knees or cut their fingers, when they get their feelings hurt, who do they run to? Mom, of course. Even wounded soldiers on the battlefield are known to cry out for their mothers in their last moments. Mother is love and tenderness and mercy. She is a picture of the heart of God.

But *identity*—especially gender identity—is bestowed by the father. A boy learns if he is a man, if he has what it takes, from his dad. A girl learns if she is worth pursuing, if she is lovely, from her dad. That's just the way God set this whole thing up. This power he has given to you.

THE VOICE OF A FATHER

On a warm August afternoon several years ago my boys and I were rock climbing in a place called Garden of the Gods near our home. We all love to climb, and our love for it goes beyond the adventure. There's something about facing a wall of rock, accepting its challenge, and mastering it that calls you out, tests, and affirms what you are made of. Besides, the boys are going to climb everything anyway—the refrigerator, the banister, the furniture—so we might as well take it outside.

My oldest son, Sam, went first. He was about eight years old at the time. Things were going well until he hit a bit of an overhang, which, even though you're roped in, makes you feel exposed and more than a little vulnerable. So I helped him up the overhang with a bit of a boost, and on he went with greater speed and confidence. "Way to go, Sam! You're looking good. That's it. Nice move! Way to go, Sam. You're a *wild man!*" He finished the climb, and as he walked down from the back side, I began to clip in his brother. Ten or fifteen minutes passed, and the story was forgotten to me. But not to Sam. While I was coaching his brother up the rock, Sam sort of sidled up to me and in a quiet voice asked, "Dad . . . did you really think I was a wild man up there?"

Miss that moment and you'll miss a boy's heart forever. It's not *a* question; it's *The* Question, the one every boy is longing to ask: "Do I have what it takes? Am I powerful?"

Until a man *knows* he's a man, he will forever be trying to prove he is one, while at the same time he will shrink from anything that might reveal he is not. Most men live their lives haunted by The Question or debilitated by the answer they've been given.

I spent a few days this fall with a very successful man I'll call Peter. He was hosting me for a conference on the East Coast, and when Peter picked me up at the airport, he was driving a new Land Rover with all the whistles and bells. *Nice car*, I thought. *This guy is doing well.* The next day we drove around in his BMW. Peter lived in the largest house in town. He had not inherited any of this wealth; he worked for every dime. He loved Formula One racing and fly-fishing for salmon in Nova Scotia. I genuinely liked him. *Now here's a man*, I said to myself.

Yet, there was something missing. You'd think a guy like that would be confident, self-assured, centered. And of course, he seemed that way at first. But as we spent time together, I found him to be . . . hesitant. He had all the appearances of masculinity, but none of it felt as though it were coming from a true center.

After several hours of conversation, he admitted he was coming to a revelation: "I lost my father earlier this year to cancer. But I did not cry when he died. You see, we were never really close."

Ah, yes, I knew what was coming next.

"All these years, knocking myself out to get ahead . . . I wasn't even enjoying myself. What was it for? I see now . . . I was trying to win my father's approval."

A long, sad silence. Then Peter said quietly, through tears, "It never worked." He never heard what he so desperately needed to hear from his dad.

You see—it's the *father* who is designed to answer our core question.

The same holds true for women. Give

your little girl a new dress and a new pair of shoes, and what will she do? Is it enough that she admires herself in the mirror? Oh, no. In a flash she'll be out there in the living room, twirling in front of her *daddy*. She wants his attention. "Am I lovely, Daddy? Am I captivating? Do you think I'm worth fighting for?"

My good friend Craig just gave his oldest daughter to be married to a fine young man. He told me afterward that the walk down the aisle with his daughter on his arm was the most beautiful and the most difficult moment of his life. He also was honored to say a few words to the bride and groom during the ceremony. As they stood there before him, the young man in a black tuxedo, standing tall and just a little bit nervous, the young woman by his side looking more beautiful than she ever has, and with a touch of apprehension in her eyes, her father spoke. He talked about her years growing up and the things that made her such a special daughter. He spoke as a father.

He paused, and with pride in his voice and love on his face, Craig said to her, "Sweetheart, you are a beautiful woman." Every woman in that church had tears in her eyes. The women were undone. Those are the very words each of them longed to hear from her father. And not just once, but a thousand times in a thousand different ways over the course of her life. *You are lovely.*

When a young woman hasn't heard this from her father, nine times out of ten she turns to a young man to try to get the answer to her question. "It's hard to be holy and passionate," a young woman confessed to me. She is a sincerely committed follower of Christ; she's also a bit more vulnerable to the boys than she'd like to be. It seems that the only way Cindy can keep from chasing after sexual intimacy with a man is to bury herself in grad school. But it doesn't seem to make the longing go away, and she soon finds herself leaving the books for another compromising situation. "Why can't I get beyond this?" she asked. "I'm praying and reading my Bible every day. But still I fall."

"What are you looking for?" I asked in return.

We sat in silence a few minutes. "I really don't know."

Her dad was not abusive, at least not in a way that would seem obvious. He was simply busy and unavailable. When he did give her his attention, it was always with a high standard of achievement. "How are your grades?" That's not what she needed to hear. She didn't want a test; she wanted to be pursued by him. "How is your *heart*?" is what she longed to hear.

Research data show that sexual promiscuity among teenage girls is almost always directly related to an absent father. And I don't necessarily mean physically absent; he might be home but emotionally withdrawn from his daughter. If he starves her for his words, his delight, his attention, she will look for those things elsewhere.

All this is to say that it is *your* voice, my friend and fellow dad, that is the most powerful voice in the world . . . in the lives of your children. No one will have the impact on them that you will have. But isn't that what you've always wanted—to be powerful? To have an eternal impact?

You do.

When it comes to what they need and what you can offer them, you have what it takes. You are the man.

THE ANSWER TO
YOUR QUESTION

Now, it's a simple fact of life that we cannot give something we don't have.

Although you may begin to see the weight of your life upon your son or daughter, at the same time you may sense a lingering doubt or fear or sense of failure inside. Because you, too, had a question growing up. You were once a boy and a young man, wondering if you had what it takes. How did your dad answer *your* question? What was his message to you, about you, as a man? Whether you are aware of it or not, that answer has shaped you into the man you are today.

Dave still remembers the day he was wounded by his father. His parents were having an argument in the kitchen, and his father was verbally abusing his mother. Dave took his mom's side, and his father exploded. "I don't remember all that was said, but I do remember his last words: 'You are such a mama's boy!' he yelled at me. Then he walked out." Perhaps if Dave had a strong relationship with his dad most of the time, a wound like that might be lessened, healed later by words of love. But the blow came after years of distance between them. Dave's father was often gone from morning till night with his own business, so they rarely spent time together. What is more, Dave felt a lingering disappointment from his dad. He wasn't a star athlete, which he knew his dad highly valued. He had a spiritual hunger and often attended church, which his dad did not value. Those words fell like a final blow, a death sentence.

How I wish it were a rare case, but I am deeply sorry to say I've heard countless stories like it. There's a young boy named Charles who loved to play the piano, but his father and brothers were jocks. One day they came back from the gym to find him at the keyboard, and who knows what else had built up years of scorn and contempt in his father's soul, but his son received both barrels: "You are such a faggot." It was devastating. Charles never played the piano again.

In the case of violent fathers, the boy's question is answered in a devastating way. "Do I have what it takes? Am I a man, Papa?" No, you are a mama's boy, an idiot, a faggot, a loser. Those are defining sentences that shape a man's life. The assault wounds are like a shotgun blast to the chest. This can get unspeakably evil when it involves physical, sexual, or verbal abuse carried on for years. Without some kind of help, many men never recover.

Other fathers give a wound merely by their silence; they are present yet absent to their sons. The silence is deafening. My father was in many ways a good man. He introduced me to the West, and he taught me to fish and to camp. I still remember the fried-egg sandwiches he made us for dinner. But like so many men of his era, my father had never faced the issues of his own wounds, and he fell to drinking when his life began to take a downhill turn. I was about eleven or twelve at the time—a very critical age in the masculine journey, the age when The Question really begins to surface. At the very moment when I was desperately wondering what it meant to be a man, and whether I had what it took, my father checked out, went silent. He had a workshop out back, attached to the garage, and he spent his hours out there alone, reading, doing crossword puzzles, and drinking. That is a major wound.

In the case of silent, passive, or absent fathers, The Question goes unanswered. "Do I have what it takes? Am I a man, Daddy?" The silence is the answer: "I don't know . . . I doubt it . . . you'll have to find out for yourself . . . probably not." The assault wounds are usually obvious. Something is shouted; something awful is done. The passive wounds are not obvious. Because they are subtle, they often go unrecognized as wounds and therefore are more difficult to heal.

But the fact remains—most fathers find it hard to validate their children, because *they* have a wound in their soul.

HEALING THE WOUNDS

Now, this booklet is about how to love your sons and daughters. I want to help you offer what they need from you. But to love them well, to fight for their hearts, you have to first get *your* heart back.

When the Bible tells us that Christ came to "redeem mankind," it means a whole lot more than forgiveness. Simply forgiving a broken man is like telling someone running a marathon, "It's okay that you've broken your leg. I won't hold that against you. Now

. . . finish the race." That is cruel to leave him wounded in that way. No, there is much more to salvation. The core of Christ's mission was foretold in Isaiah 61:

> The Spirit of the Sovereign LORD is on
> me,
> because the LORD has anointed me
> to preach good news to the poor.
> He has sent me to bind up the broken-
> hearted,
> to proclaim freedom for the captives
> and release for the prisoners. (v. 1)

The Messiah will come, he said, to bind up and heal, to release and set free. What? *Your heart.* Christ comes to restore and release you. This is *the* central passage about Jesus in the entire Bible, the one he chose to quote about himself when he stepped into the spotlight and announced his arrival (Luke 4). This is what makes Christianity such really good news. God can, and wants to, heal your heart.

How can you first find the healing of *your* wounded heart? It begins with surrender. You might remember a famous passage of Scripture that goes like this:

I stand at the door and knock. If anyone hears my voice and opens the door, I will come in. (Rev. 3:20)

It is Jesus who is speaking, and the door he refers to is the heart. He asks your permission to come in. How simple ... yet how life-changing. *You simply invite Jesus into your wound*; you ask him to come and meet you there, to enter into the broken and unhealed places of your heart. That is the first step—to take him at his word and invite Christ in, give him permission to heal all the broken places within you. Ask him to release you from all bondage and captivity, as he promised to do.

Next, you may find that you need to grieve. The wounds you received were not your fault, and they mattered. Oh, what a milestone day it was for me when I allowed myself to say that the loss of my father *mattered*. The tears that flowed were the first I'd ever granted my wound, and they were deeply healing. All those years of sucking it up melted away in my grief. It is so important for each of us to grieve our wound; it is the only honest thing to do. For in grieving we admit the truth—we were hurt by someone we loved, we lost something very dear, and it hurt us very much. Tears are healing. They help to open and cleanse the wound.

Then, you let God love you; you let him get real close to you. I know, it seems painfully obvious, but I'm telling you, few men are ever so vulnerable as to simply let themselves be loved by God.

I once asked a friend, "Brad, why don't you just let God love you?"

He squirmed in his chair. "I have such a hard time with that, just being loved. It feels so naked. I'd rather be in control."

Later he wrote me this:

After it all came crashing down, I was overwhelmed by sadness and grief. The pain is incredible. In the midst of that God asked me, "Brad, will you let me love you?" I know what he is asking. I feel anxious that I need to go e-mail all these schools and secure a future. But I'm tired of running away. I want to come home. I flipped through my Bible and came to John 15, "Just as the Father has loved you, I have also loved you; abide in my love." The battle is very intense. At times it is all clear. At others it is a fog. Right now all I can do is cling to Jesus as best

I know how and not run from all that is in my heart.

Abiding in the love of God is our only hope, the only true home for our hearts. It's not that we mentally acknowledge that God loves us. It's that we let our hearts come home to him and stay in his love. This is what another man said to me after he opened the door of his heart to Christ:

My father never left; he just never had time for me or words of encouragement. He has spent his entire life making himself the center of attention. For the first time I understand why I am highly driven, why I never let anyone get close to me—including my wife—and why I am an impostor to most people. I broke down and cried. I feel the presence of God in my heart like I have never felt him before . . . the beginning of a new heart.

And, next, you must forgive your father. Paul warned us that unforgiveness and bitterness can wreck our lives and the lives of others (Eph. 4:31; Heb. 12:15). I am sorry to think of all the years my wife endured the anger and bitterness that I redirected at her from my father. As someone has said, forgiveness is setting a prisoner free and then discovering the prisoner was you.

You must understand that forgiveness is a choice. It is not a feeling, but an act of the will. Neil Anderson has written, "Don't wait to forgive until you feel like forgiving; you will never get there. Feelings take time to heal after the choice to forgive is made." You allow God to bring the hurt up from your past, for "if your forgiveness doesn't visit the emotional core of your life, it will be incomplete." You acknowledge that it hurt, that it mattered, and you choose to extend forgiveness to your father. This is *not* saying, "It didn't really matter"; it is *not* saying, "I probably deserved part of it anyway." Forgiveness says, "It was wrong, it mattered, and I release you."

The last step is to ask God to father you and to tell you what he thinks of you.

You see, no matter how old you are, no matter how much you have (or have not) achieved, *you* still have a Question. Do *you* have what it takes? The only one who can really settle that for you is God. You must ask God. And you must stay with The Question until you get an answer. How will it be possible to validate your son or daughter when you are walking around with a huge question mark on your chest? Or worse, a gaping wound that screams, "Failure; Worthless; Crybaby!"

Oh, what wonderful stories I could tell you of how many times God has spoken to me and to other men since we've been asking The Question. My friend Aaron went to a park near our home and found a place of solitude. There he waited for the Father's voice. What he first heard was this: "True masculinity is spiritual." Aaron has for so long felt that spirituality was feminine; it put him in a terrible bind because he is a very spiritual man and yet longs to be a real man. God spoke exactly what he needed to hear— masculinity is spiritual. Then he heard, "True spirituality is good." And then, "You are a man. You are a man. You are a man."

Remember, Scripture promises that the Father's voice is *never* condemning: "There is now no condemnation for those who are in Christ Jesus" (Rom. 8:1). Whatever he has to say to you, it will not involve reproach or rejection in any way. We are forgiven. God has given each of us a new heart (Ezek. 36:26; Luke 8:15; Rom. 2:29). That is what is true. Period. From that place we ask God to speak *personally* to us, to break the power of the lie that was delivered with the wound.

IT'S NEVER TOO LATE

My father sent me a letter last year. It's a short letter, only about four sentences. Just a note, really. My dad was never long on words. He wrote it with the help of an old typewriter; ever since his stroke a few years back, his handwriting has gotten too shaky to read. Now, to be honest, it's not a particularly moving letter. He's not an eloquent man. It simply says something to the effect of "I think you are doing a great job."

I get a lot of letters. Because I'm an author, I probably receive more mail than the average guy. Over the years people have written some really encouraging things to me, and I am very grateful. But this letter from my dad is one of the few letters I've ever saved. It's one of a handful that have brought me to tears. The reason is simple. All my life I've longed to know that I, too, have what it takes. And like every other boy, I've longed to hear those words from my dad. So at the age of forty-three, a man well past my boyhood years, with my dad a gray-haired grandfather passing seventy-seven, I hang on to a few words from him.

The truth is, no matter how old your children are, they will always long to hear from you those words so central to their hearts. "You are lovely." "You have what it takes." I know—reading this little booklet has been hard for some of you. You see now that you didn't speak those words of life to your children. Maybe worse. Maybe you wounded them instead. That's a hard thing to admit. But you need to know that it isn't too late. You can still try to recover your relationship. You can still offer those words of life to them. Let me try to give some counsel on how to approach older children (high-school age and above).

Go to them. Ask them what it was like to have you as a father. Ask them what they feel your message to them was while they were growing up. Maybe it needs to start with a letter or a phone call: "I've been doing some thinking about our relationship and how I might have hurt you over the years. I'd be honored if you would tell me what it was like to have me as a dad. What was my message to you, about you, as you grew up? Did you feel loved and pursued by me (as a daughter)? Did you feel loved and respected by me (as a son)?"

43

Now, if you are blessed by God, they will tell you. It might be hard to hear. But you're a man—you can take it. Don't be quick to defend yourself. Don't rush to explain, "But those were hard years," or "I was working hard to provide for you," or whatever. Simply listen, let them speak, and then accept what they have to say. Only after the story is out on the table do you ask for their forgiveness. This is important. Don't just say you're sorry—*ask for their forgiveness*. "You're right . . . I really see that now. Will you forgive me for wounding you in that way?"

However, I need to admit that sometimes this might not go well. Your adult children might not be ready to talk to you about all of this.

Respect them. Give them time. Let them know that when they are ready, you are ready. Pray for them, that God would soften their hearts, and bring reconciliation.

Either way—and most important of all—begin to say to your children what you never said to them. *Demonstrate* your repentance. Show them you mean what you say. Begin to speak loving, affirming words to their Question. Send them cards; ask them to dinner; shoot off a quick e-mail. Not just once, but a hundred times over the next few years, tell them, "You have what it takes," or "You are lovely."

It's never too late.

THE POWER OF LOVE

I know that I have blown it with my sons. More times than I want to admit. I know that I have hurt them and will hurt them again before this whole thing is over. I am a man "under construction," undergoing renovation, and sometimes the uglier parts of me slip out. Jesus is not finished with me yet. I will never be the perfect dad. But here is what I am counting on:

Love covers over a multitude of sins.
(1 Peter 4:8)

I really want to do a great job as a dad. But
I know I will not do it perfectly. Sometimes
I'm just too tired to offer what they need;
other times I'm just plain selfish. So this verse
is what I'm banking on, more than anything
else, as a father. In the end the most important
issue is love. It always has been, always will be.
More than anything else, your son and
daughter long to know that you love them,
truly love them. That you *delight* in them. It's
really the core desire of any human heart.

You might remember that day when Jesus
was baptized by his cousin John. As he came
back out of the water, God the Father
spoke—I mean, literally, out loud, so every-
one could hear. He did that only three times
in the entire life of Christ, so it must have
been an important moment. What did the
Father have to say?

This is My beloved Son, in whom I am well pleased. (Matt. 3:17 NKJV)

In other words, "Jesus, you are my delight. I am so very proud of you. You have what it takes." God the Father expressed his delight in his Son. This is just amazing. There's our model—there's the basic message that we, too, are meant to give our children: "I delight in you." Somehow when a child is secure in that love, the wounds just don't go quite as deep, and the lesser failings are more easily forgotten.

This is the most basic of all our missions, the fundamental assignment of our lives: to make sure our children know that we love them. To say to each son, "I'm so proud of you. You have what it takes." To let each daughter know, "How I delight in you. You are lovely." If we get that said, and said a thousand different ways over the course of their childhoods, we'll have done a pretty good job of being dads.

Every dad can offer this.

But only *you* can offer this as a father to your children. You are the man.

You have what it takes.

IF YOU WANT MORE

This booklet was drawn from some key ideas in a book I wrote titled *Wild at Heart: Discovering the Secret of a Man's Soul*. If anything I have said here has touched a nerve, awakened you to the weight of your life, I really want to encourage you to get a fuller understanding by reading *Wild at Heart* for yourself.

You might also find it helpful to have alongside the *Wild at Heart Field Manual*, a sort of workbook I wrote to help men bring these truths deep into their own hearts and to discover the healing and the validation God has for them.

My prayer is that your heart would be restored, and having found that from God, you would be able to offer it to those you love.

ABOUT THE AUTHOR

John Eldredge is the founder and director of Ransomed Heart™ Ministries in Colorado Springs, Colorado, a fellowship devoted to helping people recover and live from their deep heart. John is the author of numerous books, including *Waking the Dead, Wild at Heart, The Sacred Romance,* and *The Journey of Desire.* John lives in Colorado with his wife, Stasi, and their three sons, Samuel, Blaine, and Luke. He is an avid outdoorsman who loves being in the wild.

To learn more about John's seminars, audiotapes, and other resources for the heart, visit him on the Web at:

www.RansomedHeart.com

Or, write

Ransomed Heart™ Ministries

P.O. Box 51065

Colorado Springs, Co. 80949-1065

ALSO AVAILABLE FROM
JOHN ELDREDGE

———◦►———

WAKING THE DEAD

In *Waking the Dead,* John Eldredge shows how God restores your heart, your true humanity, and sets you free. There are four streams, Eldredge says, through which you can discover the abundant life: Walking with God, Receiving His Intimate Counsel, Deep Restoration, and Spiritual Warfare. And once the "eyes of your heart" are opened, you will embrace three eternal truths: Things are not what they seem; This is a world at war; and You have a crucial role to play. A battle is raging. And it is a battle for your heart.

Hardcover—ISBN 0-7852-6553-8
Abridged Audio in 3 CDs—ISBN 0-7852-6299-7

A GUIDEBOOK TO WAKING THE DEAD

In a style similar to *The Journey of Desire Journal and Guidebook,* Eldredge and Craig McConnell lead you on a journey toward a restored heart, true humanity, and ultimate freedom.

ISBN 0-7852-6309-8

WILD AT HEART

Every man was once a boy. And every little boy has dreams, big dreams. But what happens to those dreams when they grow up? In *Wild at Heart,* John Eldredge invites men to recover their masculine heart, defined in the image of a passionate God. And he invites women to discover the secret of a man's soul and to delight in the strength and wildness men were created to offer.

Hardcover—ISBN 0-7852-6883-9
Abridged Audio in 3 CDs—ISBN 0-7852-6298-9
Abridged Audio in 2 Cassettes—ISBN 0-7852-6498-1
Spanish Edition (*Salvaje de Corazón*)—ISBN 0-8811-3716-2

WILD AT HEART FIELD MANUAL

Abandoning the format of workbooks-as-you-know-them, the *Wild at Heart Field Manual* will take you on a journey through which you will receive permission to be what God designed you to be—dangerous, passionate, alive, and free. Filled with questions, exercises, personal stories from readers, wide-open writing spaces to record your "field notes," this book will lead you on a journey to discover the masculine heart that God gave you.

ISBN 0-7852-6574-0

WILD AT HEART: A BAND OF BROTHERS

Five friends. Eight days. No scripts. Here's what it looks like to live the message of *Wild at Heart* in a band of real brothers. John and his band of brothers spent eight days shooting this series on a ranch in Colorado. Horses. Rappelling. White-water rafting. Fly-fishing. And some of the most honest conversation you will ever hear from men. This is not a scripted instructional video. It is real life and conversation shared with the cameras rolling. If you're looking for more, this is the next step in the *Wild at Heart* adventure for you and your band of brothers. The Multi-Media Facilitator's Kit includes John's best-selling *Wild at Heart* hardcover book; the *Wild at Heart Field Manual;* the *Wild at Heart Facilitator's Guide;* the video teaching series available either in VHS or DVD format; and a media kit to help you get the word out so others can join your band of brothers.

VHS ISBN 1-4002-0087-3
DVD ISBN 1-4002-0086-5

THE WILD AT HEART JOURNAL

This rugged leather-bound guided journey will help men explore their hearts and journal their adventures. This includes totally different material than that found in the *Field Manual*.

ISBN 0-8499-5763-X

THE JOURNEY OF DESIRE

Author Dan Allender calls *The Journey of Desire* "a profound and winsome call to walk into the heart of God." This life-changing book picks up where *The Sacred Romance* leaves off and continues the journey. In it, John Eldredge invites you to abandon resignation, to rediscover your God-given desires, and to search again for the life you once dreamed of.

Hardcover Edition—ISBN 0-7852-6882-0
Trade Paper Edition—ISBN 0-7852-6716-6

THE JOURNEY OF DESIRE JOURNAL AND GUIDEBOOK

John Eldredge, with Craig McConnell, offers a unique, thought-provoking, and life-recapturing workbook, which invites you to rediscover your God-given desire and to search again for the life you once dreamed of. Less of a workbook and more of a flowing journal, this book includes personal responses to questions from John and Craig.

ISBN 0-7852-6640-2

THE SACRED ROMANCE

This life-changing book by Brent Curtis and John Eldredge has guided hundreds of thousands of readers from a busyness-based religion to a deeply felt relationship with the God who woos you. As you draw closer to Him, you must choose to let go of other "less-wild lovers," such as perfectionistic drivenness and self-indulgence, and embark on your own journey to recover the lost life of your heart and with it the intimacy, beauty, and adventure of life with God.

Trade Paper Edition—ISBN 0-7852-7342-5
Special Collector's Edition (Hardcover)—ISBN 0-7852-6723-9
Abridged Audio in 2 Cassettes—ISBN 0-7852-6786-7
Spanish Edition *(El Sagrado Romance)*—ISBN 0-8811-3648-4

THE SACRED ROMANCE WORKBOOK AND JOURNAL

John Eldredge offers a guided journey of the heart featuring exercises, journaling, and the arts to usher you into an *experience*—the recovery of your heart and the discovery of your life as part of God's great romance.

ISBN 0-7852-6846-4

THE THREE CLASSICS

The Sacred Romance, The Journey of Desire, and *Wild at Heart* are available in one specially priced package. Whether this set is for yourself, to replace the dog-eared and penciled-in copies you already own, or is a gift to share John's powerful message with someone you love, these *Three Classics from John Eldredge* will continue to give long after they are received.

ISBN 0-7852-6635-6

DARE TO DESIRE

Complete with beautiful, full-color design, *Dare to Desire* is the perfect book if you are ready to move beyond the daily grind to a life overflowing with adventure, beauty, and a God who loves you more passionately than you dared imagine. With brand-new content as well as concepts from *The Sacred Romance, The Journey of Desire,* and *Wild at Heart,* John Eldredge takes you on a majestic journey through the uncharted waters of the human heart.

ISBN 0-8499-9591-4